i

Bill Gates:
The Man Behind Microsoft

Bill Gates:
The Man Behind Microsoft

A Look at the Man

Who Changed the World We Live In

JR MacGregor

Bill Gates: The Man Behind Microsoft

A Look at the Man Who Changed the World We Live In

Published by CAC Publishing LLC.

ISBN 978-1-948489-86-7 paperback

ISBN 978-1-948489-85-0 eBook

This book is dedicated to those who want to study and learn from one of the greatest visionaries that has ever walked this planet.

Contents

Preface

It is challenging to write about a man who is recognized the world over. The challenge is not in finding data and narrative, but is in finding something that has not already been said or something that has not already become part of the reading public's collective consciousness. Ultimately, the real challenge is not in finding something to write about Bill Gates, but in telling the truth of the man amid the rumors, bias, confusion, and exaggeration.

We tend to emulate our heroes in one thing or another. That is the underlying reason we look at biographies of great or prominent men. Some will look at Bill Gates primarily because of his ranking at the apex of the Forbes list for 24 years in a row. But this book is not about the fact that Bill Gates has sat on the top of a variety of Forbes' lists. The success we are looking at here is not about the wealth that he has amassed. Any discussion of the quantity of wealth or the price of MSFT's stock price tends to minimize the real benefit of the lessons we can take away from Bill Gates' story.

So, let's set fortunes aside, and boil down our discussion of Bill Gates to just two things we can focus our attention on. The first are his strengths and weaknesses in mind and body. The other is what inspires him and his overarching views about life and his place in it.

This narrative has two parallel objectives. One is simply to satisfy our curiosity about the success of one man whose vision has touched billions of lives in this generation and will continue to touch countless more in coming generations. The second is to strip away the noise that skews the description of the effort and energy that went into accomplishing what Bill Gates has done.

For Bill Gates, the effort was not about the rewards and riches. After all, once you get to a certain point, rewards do get boring. If you stood at the banks of a pristine lake, how much of it could you really drink in this lifetime? Ultimately, it is not about the rewards or their accumulation. It isn't about the status, or whatever power that brings with it. The real glory is in seeing how much you have used your time here on this earth to make a difference.

If you make enough of a difference, then the reward lies within what you have accomplished. The key to understand those who have truly accomplished their vision is that the rewards are not their primary motivation. They don't start out with fantasies of golden towers and luxurious lifestyles.

Ones who are truly inspired don't need to be showered with lavish ornaments. Those who do need that are often the ones who don't really contribute anything in return for the rewards they gain (or sometimes steal). Emperor Nero is a famous example.

In my book on Jack Ma, founder of the Chinese business giant Alibaba, I describe how, when he first ventured out on his own to start a translation business, he had to work a second job selling odds and ends at a market outside his city just to keep the lights on at his fledgling business. His translation business finally turned the corner after three years. If it had been only about the money, Ma would have quit long before then.

In the same way, Bill Gates quit Harvard (with its rewards) so that he could devote all his attention to his passion. Harvard would have been the wiser choice—from a conventional perspective. Most would see admission into Harvard as a one-way ticket to an easy life at a lucrative job at an investment bank or at some other cushy job. Instead of slogging his way through the first three years of Harvard College, Bill Gates took the inspired step to focus full time on his start up.

In leaving Harvard, Gates wasn't making a decision that some imagined pursuit of fame and glory outweighed the value of a strong education. Instead, he calculated his options, and, for him, his decision to pursue his dream was a logical one. Bill Gates was not the type to take risks. When he left Harvard, he had a little over year to graduate and didn't yet have the IBM contract in hand, but he did have a clear vision of what he wanted to do. (I can just imagine the conversation my parents would have had at the kitchen table that night, if I had called to say I was quitting Harvard to pursue what had been, until that point, only a hobby.) But Gates was a very straightforward person with no theatrics prior to a decision—and no regrets after it.

At first, we might look into a person's biography out of curiosity, but that curiosity really comes from a deeper desire to find similarities between that person's life and our own. When we are young, we look for heroes to emulate; when we get a little older, the flavor of those heroes evolves along with our age and maturity. Our heroes change, and the aspect of their lives that we want to emulate also changes.

When I was a kid, I wanted to be Steve Austin—the original Six Million Dollar Man. I wanted to be the astronaut who went down in a blaze of glory and was rebuilt with superhuman strength and power. In time, that changed, and my heroes went from the fantastical, like Steve Austin, to the commercial giants, like Mike Milken and Gordon Gecko.

A person's heroes reveal who they are built to be, not that our lives are preordained, but that we have the tools that makes one path easier to navigate than another. Take, for instance, Mark Zuckerberg, the founder of Facebook—as a kid, his hero was Bill Gates. And look at the path Zuckerberg was to excel at.

To really fulfill and wake up the giant within you, you need to get beyond the motivations of reward and look for motivation in contribution and achievement. Most men of great accomplishment do this, and it pays off in the end. Bill Gates did this from the beginning. He had no utility for money or wealth in the way we normally fantasize about. What we really hope for is the freedom to do whatever we want, with the imagined liberation that wealth brings.

Eventually, abundance of wealth and accomplishment come to those who aren't focusing on the reward but are totally and absolutely focused on their contribution. That is the mark of a person who has truly earned every penny.

Most of the men I study and write about—Steve Jobs, Jeff Bezos, Richard Branson, Jack Ma, and others— have this one thing in common: they were not mentally spending their money before they have worked for their achievement with their hands. Each of them has followed the path laid out in the books I have written in the success series.

Introduction

Bill Gates was born William Henry Gates on October 28, 1955 in Seattle, Washington to William Henry Gates, Sr. and Mary Maxwell Gates.

To understand Bill Gates and the nature of his accomplishments, we must look to the environment he was a part of—his father, mother, siblings, grandparents, and the kinds of friends and extended family he was exposed to. The success story of Bill Gates did not happen in a vacuum; his background, the powerful parents he had, the time he was born into, and the town he grew up in, each played their parts.

Both of Bill Gates' parents, Senior and Mary, had prominent roles in the modern development of Seattle and Washington, and were, in their own rights, respected names in the state.

Bill Gates' father, William Henry Gates, Sr. (originally named William Henry Gates III), was an attorney and shifted his primary focus to philanthropy upon retirement. Not just "father of the co-founder of Microsoft," Gates Senior has been one of the most accomplished Americans alive today—in his own right.

Bill Gates, Sr. was born in 1927 in Bremerton, Washington, a town just west of Seattle across Puget Sound. He grew up in Bremerton in a simple and loving home. His father owned and operated a furniture store that he later sold. After the store was sold, Senior's father continued to work in the furniture industry. It was a time and place where honor, respect, and accomplishment were part of one's lifestyle. Senior was raised in a loving home that was firm and focused on an honest day's work for an honest day's wage. A deep sense of nationalism, pride in one's country and their own northwest culture pervaded the community.

The town of Bremerton was the home to the Puget Sound Naval Shipyard. In World War II, the shipyard played an important role in America's naval efforts. It was the key location in the Pacific for the maintenance and repair of battle-damaged ships for the entire US Pacific fleet, and everyone growing up there had a very personal experience of World War II. After the Pearl Harbor attack, it became conceivable that the US west coast could be a target too, and there were nightly blackouts. While most of the United States was at an arm's length from the war, Bremerton, and other towns like it in the Pacific Northwest, faced the war in a very real way.

Bill Gates, Sr. attended Bremerton High which he graduated from in 1943. A year later, he was ordered to enlist for active duty. He joined the US Army and went through officer's training. Shortly after, he was shipped out to Japan where he spent time in Tokyo and war-torn Hokkaido. After, Senior returned to Puget Sound and attended the University of Washington where he earned his undergraduate degree in 1949 and his law degree in 1950.

Bill Gates, Sr. returned to Bremerton to take up the position of assistant city attorney. As his distinguished law career unfolded, it moved toward the corporate world, and, in particular, the world of technology.

Nearby Seattle was the original natural incubator for new ideas and new technology. Bill Gates, Sr. and his law firm worked with the cutting-edge technologies that were sprouting up in the prosperous days following WWII. Senior found himself at the intersection of technology, commerce, and law, which gave him a front row seat overlooking the areas of ascendency that would lead the United States into decades of prosperity. For instance, the barcodes we still take for granted at the grocery store checkout were a technological revolution brought out by a Washington company that was a client of the firm Senior worked at. To this day, one can find Senior's fingerprints on a number of successful ventures in the Washington-Pacific Northwest area and across the United States. Over the years, his law firm evolved and is now known as K&L Gates.

Meanwhile, on the home front, Bill Gates, Sr. had met and was dating Mary Maxwell, also a UW student, two years his junior, before Senior left for Japan. They were married in 1951, after he returned.

Mary Maxwell came from the upper echelons of Washington society. Her father, James Willard Maxwell, Jr., was a prominent banker in the Pacific Northwest. Her grandfather, James Willard Maxwell, was also a respected banker in the west, and served on the board of the American Automobile Association and on the Seattle Chamber of Commerce.

Mary Maxwell Gates, herself, served on the Board of Regents for the University of Washington for 18 years before passing from breast cancer in 1994. She also sat on the boards of United Way and the First Interstate BancSystem.

Bill Gates, Sr. and Mary Gates had three children, Bill Gates and his two sisters, Kristianne (Kristi) and Elizabeth (Libby). Kristi Gates, the oldest of the three siblings, born in 1954, graduated from the University of Washington and is now a CPA. She also sits on the Board of Regents for the University of Washington. Libby Gates, the youngest, was born in in 1964. She is currently a social activist living in Seattle. She graduated from Pomona College with a degree in Economics.

Chapter 1 Childhood

"Many of our deepest motives come, not from an adult logic of how things work in the world, but out of something that is frozen from childhood."

Kazuo Ishiguro

Bill Gates has retained most of the qualities he had as a child into his adulthood. Looking at his childhood provides insight into how Bill Gates developed and into the two forces that have played a major roles in his life, family and humanitarianism.

Let us start with how his family influenced Bill Gates' childhood. Looking at my own childhood, or the childhoods of most people I know, I would not be able to find one story that remotely resembles the childhood that Bill Gates had.

First, from early on, Bill was remarkably mature for his age. His maturity had everything to do with having a very stable thought process. Bill never had any of the problems in how or when he spoke that most kids have (most kids have the innate ability to put their feet into their mouths).

Second, even for young Bill Gates, fairness came in explicit form. The more formal the statement of terms and benefits, the more fair and equitable it was. If it was not reduced to paper, and, if it was not equitable, all bets were off. To ensure this, he used to sign agreements with his siblings for various promises.

Third, Bill Gates observed his father's actions and motivations intently. Senior was all about the oneness of humanity. While Bill Gates, Sr. had been posted to Japan after the war, he had seen, first-hand, the devastation that lay in the wake of a war. For most Americans, the war had been an ocean away, whether east or west, but, for Gates Senior, his experience of the effects of the war, and the condition it leaves humanity in, resonated so powerfully and loudly throughout his life that it spilled over and touched his son.

Gates Senior projected an imprint onto young Bill in three areas that were to feature prominently in Bill Gates' own life: Senior's empathy, affinity for technology, and definition of equitability.

The other force that steered Bill Gates' childhood was his mother, Mary. Bill's relationship with his mother was close and complex. Young Gates learned as much from his mother as he did from his father.

There was a sense of ambition and competition that he learnt from his mother and his maternal grandfather. He learned from the stories about James Willard Maxwell, Jr. that Mary Gates and her mother told Bill. Overall, he could see the forces of his banker grandfather manifested in his mother and he absorbed a lot of their instincts and powers.

Bill's mother, Mary Gates, was well known in King's County for her ability to organize and socialize. Those skills didn't necessarily come naturally to Bill Gates, but later he found that shortcoming (if you can call it that) nicely compensated for by Melinda, his wife. In many areas where Bill comes up short, Melinda has been the one to carry it across the finish line.

Gam, Bill's maternal grandmother, was also a major influence in his life, as the Gates children were often left in her care. She was a hard-driving woman who pushed them to excel and fostered a strong sense of competitiveness in her grandchildren with games and athletic contests.

Bill Gates was not at all what you might imagine he would have been as a kid. He was not the quiet "geeky" type who was too meek to get out into the real world, far from it. He was more than well-adjusted. He simply happened to like programming and was good at it.As a child, he had a lot of spunk, and was quite the mischievous sort, a lot like Mark Twain's Tom Sawyer.

Even as a child, Bill Gates had a way about him that many misunderstand, mistaking it for arrogance. For example, when he was ten years old, and in an apparent bout of exasperation with his mother, he asked her if she was ever able to think things through. At the time he said it, he meant it literally the way he said it, but to anyone overhearing, it would have seemed extremely rude and impolite. But that was Bill—he had no time for niceties and polite discourse. He has always needed to get to the point and make sure the other person was on board right away.

Bill Gates was certainly academically advanced, but that didn't mean he didn't get into his share of trouble in his youth. Even in childhood, Bill failed to see the world the way the rest of us are inculcated into seeing it. Along with ambition and freedom to think came a lack of adherence to rules. Not so much a lack of respect for authority, it had more to do with not being able to see the point of the rule in question. As a child, he did not think that the rules applied to people like him.

As a kid, Bill was quite the hacker. He had the smarts to do it, he learned the tools to execute it, and he was fearless to pull it off. He hacked numerous computers as a kid—and those are just the ones he has talked about. While hacking, generally, may be frowned upon, there are many kinds of hacking. The one thing all hackers needed, especially back when the tools for hacking were not as prevalent as they are today, was the intelligence to do it. And Bill Gates has that genius.

Later, even though Gates understood that there was a law that set limits on driving speed, he wouldn't keep to speed limits. To him, there are two aspects to that law. First, the law existed to protect the public from people who were not so smart and did not really know how to drive or didn't have the skill to be safe at higher speeds. In his mind, he was obviously not in that group. However, his speeding was not without accidents. He once took a friend's Porsche and severely damaged it, just pennies below the definition of "totaled." Ultimately, his lack of respect for authority got him a ton of speeding tickets, so many he ended up in court and had to engage a lawyer to sort it out.

Even once he was at Harvard College, he was known to spend nights playing poker. His poker days, when he lost thousands at a time, were not exactly within campus rules. They played across the halls, but on the quiet. Yet, as he spent nights playing poker, Bill Gates was learning two things more effectively than any classroom could ever teach him.

First, playing poker, Gates learned how to assess risk. It is one thing to understand probability, statistics, and risk. It is a completely different thing to develop a knack for it and the understanding to overcome it. His hands at poker on Harvard Yard brought him up-close and personal with the realities of risk. He came to understand that to make anything of himself, he needed to embark on endeavors where he could control and mitigate risk. He never let go of a sure footing until he knew he had something to cling on to. This intimate understanding of risk prepared him for the way he would go out into the world and conduct business.

Gates had learned about risk in an up-close and personal way and had paid for that lesson time and time again. Later, in his dealings with IBM, he would demonstrate the lessons he had learned in how to handle business in a risk-averse manner. He showed IBM the operating system but did not buy it from the original developers until he knew the deal was a sure thing. Gates had hedged his bets.

The second thing Gates learned from playing poker during those nights at Harvard was the skill of bluffing. Bluffing is what poker is all about. If you don't know how to bluff, there are two things you should never do. First, you should never play poker. Second, you should not go into business for yourself. Bluffing allows you to control the dynamics and information flow in a negotiation.

Some may consider bluffing to be the cousin of lying and cheating. No. It is not. Is it lying and cheating to tell your mom that her bland pot roast tastes delicious? Is it lying and cheating to tell your wife that her new hairdo is fantastic? Or is it lying and cheating to tell your significant other you have a headache? Those are all bluffs done in the pursuit of bridging the gap. On the other hand, if you steal someone's technology and resell it without paying for it, that would be cheating and lying.

Bill Gates' childhood is peppered with incidents that reveal his ability to think independently and behave outside the norms of society. But even though he marched to the beat of his own drum, he was not into harming others intentionally. He was simply so sure of himself that he believed in all earnestness that the norms and laws of common people didn't apply to him.

Remember—one of the ways to succeed in life is to break a few rules, redefine your reality, and engineer your chances. Bill Gates knows this concept very well.

While he was in high school, he was hired by the faculty to do some programming for the administration. He did what was asked, but he also hacked the system to put himself into a class where he was the only guy—the rest were all girls. If you were to ask a teacher, an administrator, or a headmaster if that was the wrong thing to do, they are likely to say it was—but it didn't do any harm. However, the episode reveals a lot about Bill Gates' relationship with risk and reward. He understood keenly that, by reducing his competition, he tipped the chances in his favor. Most of us have probably thought of doing similar things, but we didn't because either we didn't have the skill to pull it off or we didn't have the guts to put our skill to use.

Bill Gates was a tough boy and strong-headed in many ways, but he had his fears. Unlike most kids, his fears didn't revolve around stories of monsters and bugs; Bill Gates' fears were about not winning. He was the kind of person that needed to win everything and be at the top. For him, winning was his paramount purpose in life, and, whatever he did, wherever he went, the thing that was on his mind was how he would win the day.

In the Gates household, everything was about ambition and hard work. It all boiled down to competition. The notion of competition in the Gates family was somewhat different than it would be in most families. It was the norm in the Gates family to compete for everything. Senior and Mary made it a point to instill a competitive spirit in their children because they believed that competition, above all else, was the mother of success. Often, competition was more important than the outcome, but the winner was always rewarded, and the loser was always made to compensate the loss.

That competitive nature was a universal for young Bill. He applied competition to everything, to every program he wrote, to every race he entered. In every shadow in his mind, there was competition.

His nights of poker in college were also about competition. Sure, it was about money, but not as much as it was about winning the challenge and emerging victorious in the moment. Poker evolved into a competition of wits. The smarter person, the person better able to bluff, became the winner. To win this affirmation, no amount of money was too much.

Consider, for example, Gates' contempt for sleep. It was well-known among his friends that Bill was a night owl. That was when he would do his work and get things done. Even after Microsoft was founded, he would go days without sleep, then crash on the office floor for a nap before getting up and getting back to whatever had been fully occupying his consciousness.

He was always on a mission to get the task or the job done; Gates was competing against time which was always against him. That was the way he knew to do things so that he could win the competition being played out in his mind. His contempt for sleep was more about winning that competition than about anything else.

Gates' contempt for sleep, and for anything else that would distract him from what he was trying to accomplish, was the result of his uncommonly singular focus. His ability to get into a program and pull it to pieces before putting it together again was not without challenges. The only thing that got him through those times, as they do today, was his ability to do just one thing at one time.

He would not allow anything to shake his focus or distract him from accomplishing whatever he had set out to do. That was the only reason that he was able to go without sleep. That was also the reason it was so difficult to tear him away, even to meet someone important for dinner. Bill Gates simply chooses to apply his time differently than the rest of us.

What would it be like to have the kind of focus and strength to continue focusing on something as you grow increasingly tired? Most people can only keep their attention on something for 5-6 minutes, and then they are done. Their focus wanes and they get distracted. It is a fact of life. It is almost superhuman to be able to focus on things for extended periods of time, yet, that is something that came easily to Bill Gates.

***

Chapter 2 Mother's Influence

"There is no influence so powerful as that of the mother"

Sarah Joseph Hale

There are many ways Mary Maxwell Gates contributed to her son's personal development and life, but she was also behind some decisive moments in Bill Gates' history. Many people don't realize that it was Mary Gates who was responsible for introducing Bill Gates to Warren Buffet—whom Bill had referred to, at the time, as someone of no value and as a person who sold pieces of paper having no value. She was also instrumental in helping Bill get the meeting with IBM that turned the table for his start-up company, Microsoft.

Bill Gates' mother was a force to be reckoned with in her own right. As prominent as Gates Senior, Mary Gates stood right alongside Senior doing her own thing and powering through the community under her own steam. She was a well-respected philanthropist and socialite, and a member on several prominent boards. Just before she passed away, she was scheduled to receive the Citizen of the Year Award for her contribution to the local community in Kings County. Her activities in the county and the state had by then spanned more than two decades.

Mary's social calendar blended with her philanthropy, and Bill Gates had a front row seat to observe the way she did things. She was as objective-oriented as her husband, Gates Senior, and she was just as forceful in getting things done. It is no wonder that Bill Gates became as tenacious as she had been throughout her life.

At first, a quality that did not pass down to Bill Gates was Mary Gates' ability to socialize. Bill found it a waste of time. The first time Mary Gates invited Warren Buffet to their home in Seattle and asked Bill to join them, Bill refused. Eventually, however, she persuaded him to come, extracting his promise to spend two hours before heading back to the office. Bill ended up spending the entire evening and late into the night.

Because of her social skill and penchant for organizing community events, Mary Gates rose to the top of the United Way Board in Kings County, eventually leading it. That gave her a stepping stone to get onto the board of United Way at the national level, and she eventually became the first woman to head it. That was to prove extremely well-timed and fortuitous for Bill.

Just around the time Mary was President of the United Way, Bill Gates was pulling his startup together. Microsoft was coming together, but not as fast as he would have liked. He was working hard, and there was a lot of good he was doing, but it was nowhere close to enough. During one of her United Way board meetings in 1980, Mary Gates spoke with a fellow board member, John Opel, the Chairman of IBM, and mentioned her son, Bill—and Microsoft.

John Opel took that back to the other executives at IBM. They called Bill Gates in about the operating system he had pitched to them sometime earlier. Not long after, Microsoft was awarded the contract to write the DOS program for all the IBM personal computers. That was Microsoft's big break.

Until then, Bill Gates and Paul Allen were just another small software programming company without a long term major client. They did have some large clients before that, but nothing on this scale. IBM's decision to award the operating system contract to Microsoft is what catapulted the company to where it is today.

Earlier, when Bill had decided to make the pitch, he didn't have any operating system (OS) to offer IBM, but he did know of someone who did. So, he took that software and offered it to IBM for evaluation.

IBM tested the OS and found that it worked as they intended, requiring only a few tweaks. So, they agreed to have Microsoft to do it. Microsoft then went to the original owners and purchased the rights to the operating system. The company pulled together all it could and paid the original developers the agreed price. Once the purchase of the software was secured and paid for, Bill Gates signed that pivotal contract licensing the software to IBM. The rest, as they say, is history.

Mary Gates also had a hand in setting up her son to meet the man who was to become one of Bill's best friends—and an important ally in his later philanthropic efforts. Bill Gates and Warren Buffet remain the best of friends to this day, chit-chatting, and going to McDonalds for burgers. It would be fascinating to watch and eavesdrop on the conversation of these two titans of the business and philanthropic world.

***

Chapter 3 Father's Guidance

"My dad expanded his horizons way beyond what he grew up with"

Bill Gates

Whoever else a man has a relationship with, be it sibling, best friend, mother, wife, or child, what has a larger bearing on who the man becomes, for good or bad, is the relationship he has with his father and the kind of man his father is. This influence is more than evident in the relationship between Bill Gates, Sr. and Bill Gates.

Most of the lessons Bill Gates learned from his father were not ones that Senior needed to sit Bill down to drill into him. Instead, Bill's lessons in life were provided by example. In a home dominated by women, Bill's focus and attention on how to become a man was trained squarely on his father. Senior was a silent and powerful force in the development of his son. Gates Senior was a man who thought before he spoke, evaluated before he acted, and made his position known in as few words as possible. His moral authority spoke for him. And Senior's empathy for humanity and all things was the path that young Bill Gates followed.

There is no doubt his lawyer father had a strong influence on Bill Gates. At an age when most kids were playing sticks and stones and taking their sibling's things without permission, young Bill (or Trey, as he was called at home) was drafting contracts for the use and borrowing of his things or his sisters' belongings. He'd write up a contract and have his sister, or whoever he was dealing with at the time, sign it, and he would work off the contract. He never deviated from the terms of the legal paper.

You have no desire to go off the rails when you are always in the shadow of a man who does the right thing—not one who simply professes to do the right thing or claims to be the best, but one who quietly does the right thing—and that becomes apparent for the world to see. Bill Gates experienced this first hand and was molded by it.

Bill Gates Senior was a powerful presence, towering over everyone at six feet seven inches, but his intellectual honesty and moral authority tower much higher.

When you come face to face with someone like Gates Senior, you are instantly subjected to a moral authority that is uncommon these days. His air, his words, his presence all just make you want to do the right thing without hesitation. There is a moral authority that comes when a person is on the right side of events and on the proper side of choices. It creates an unmistakable sense of authority that resonates.

We have already mentioned Bill Gates Senior's connection to barcode technology. There are many other similar stories about Senior's role in iconic American institutions. One of them—about what may be your favorite coffee place (certainly, it is mine)— illustrates the Senior Gates' powerful presence and his influence on events and people—something the younger Gates grew up observing.

In 1982, a man named Howard Schultz stepped into a local Starbucks, at a time when there were only six stores anywhere. He loved it so much that he pursued a meeting with the owners to persuade them to give him a job. They hired him a year later. He had a good time, but eventually outgrew the then-small Starbucks and found an Italian brand on one of his trips. Schultz brought that brand back to the United States and set up Il Giornale.

In 1987, Jerry Baldwin, the founder of Starbucks, decided to sell the six stores for a total of $3.8 million, and the first person he thought of was Howard Schultz. Baldwin called Schultz to give him a 90 day exclusive to raise the money for the purchase. Schultz agreed.

Two months into the process, Schultz got a call informing him that one of the investors of Il Giornale had made an all-cash offer topping out at $4 million. It was to be a straight forward no-due-diligence deal that would put money into Baldwin's pockets right away. The offer was too good to refuse.

Schultz was devastated and disclosed the matter to a friend who was a lawyer. That friend told Schultz to come in and meet his senior partner who might be able to help. Howard Schultz was about to meet Gates Senior.

Senior listened intently to the whole story, and, at the end, got up and signaled, as he got his coat, for Schultz to follow him. They walked across downtown Seattle to the office of the man who had made the offer.

When Gates Senior and Howard Schultz got to the office of the competing buyer, Senior spoke to the buyer directly and without hesitation, telling him to back off the attempted purchase. There was no threats, no condescension, and no hostility. All Senior had in his arsenal was the will and power to make things happen. Senior was a force in that way.

Howard Schultz went on to buy Starbucks, consisting of those first six stores, and grew it to over 20,000 stores worldwide serving millions of customers speaking dozens of languages. It is safe to say that the iconic coffee chain would not be what it is today were it not for the ability of Bill Gates, Sr. to move mountains.

Senior had a way about him that could make anything happen—and that was one of the many characteristics he passed on to become part of the younger Bill Gates. While Senior was a force that you could feel naturally, Bill Gates had to work at emulating the qualities and traits of his father. And he did.

When Apple Computer CEO and founder, Steve Jobs, hired Microsoft to build the software that Apple needed for its new line, Bill Gates saw the work that Steve Jobs was doing and advised him to acquire the code behind the point-and-click-based operating system. Jobs declined because he was focusing on the hardware, not the software.

So, when Gates returned to Seattle in November 1983, he announced that Microsoft would introduce a "Windows" based system. Two years later, Windows was released. It became global phenomenon, extending Microsoft's winning streak far beyond the success of the MS-DOS operating system. Gates had seized an open opportunity, working off a project that had no copyright issues. He didn't cheat anyone out of anything—he just stuck to the contract.

The older Gates also had a sense of social responsibility that was to become an even greater part of how his son, Bill Gates, does things today.

Bill Gates, Sr. took an active role in his local community. He had once been advised by a gathering of up and coming leaders that the most fulfilling and satisfying thing anyone could do was to take part in community development. He knew one thing to be true, and it was that we are all here to actively develop our shared space and time. But he did not have to beat the drum about it. There was no air of superiority about him over his philanthropic activities, only humility. Knowing that he and his family were drivers of social development did not make him feel anything but honored to have the opportunity.

His ardent belief that every life is of equal value has been one of the driving forces of Senior's life, and that legacy has been carried forward into the life of Bill Gates as well. The Bill and Melinda Gates Foundation, which Bill co-founded with his wife, does philanthropic work around the world. Bill and Melinda have personally donated more than $28 billion to its efforts. Of that, more than $8 billion has been primarily for health infrastructure.

A clearer example could not exist of the continuity between the way Senior sees things and the way Bill does things. His civic mindedness dictated acts beyond charity. Senior was a powerful advocate and force in the philanthropic community. Senior championed everything from the United Way to Planned Parenthood and state tax initiatives.

Bill Gates has been no different, as evidenced by the depth of involvement their Foundation has had in communities around the world. In total, the Foundation is responsible for over $48 billion dollars, and has offices in Asia, East Asia, Africa, and the Americas. It is a well-structured and highly serious organization that oversees the health and welfare of those left behind by the imperfect organization of societies. Bill and Melinda are driven by the same principal, when it comes to their foundation, as Senior has been—that everyone's life is of equal value.

On top of that, the younger Bill Gates did not just happen to stumble upon programming and technology. He didn't start to look at programming, computers, and technology in a vacuum. Technology was such an important part of Gates Senior's professional life that Senior can be found at the point of genesis for many of the tech and biotech industries that we see today. Senior and a handful of people clearly understood the utility that technology would have in the development and advancement of everyone. Bill Gates got to know the world of technological innovation through watching his father. Then, as children sometimes do, Bill picked up on it and took it further, but the original spark came from Senior.

Two divergent narratives about Bill Gates have made their way around blogs and the internet. Both the ones that demonize Gates by talking about how undeserving Gates is and the ones that exalt him as a boy from a simple family who grew up to dominate the world of software are wrong. Bill Gates needs to be seen as the product of his childhood, as a man who developed under the example and guidance of a towering figure in Washington state's history, his father.

***

Chapter 4 A Character to Emulate

"I believe that if you show people the problems and you show them the solutions they will be moved to act."

Bill Gates

It is unrealistic and even dangerous to imitate the ways and means of a single person in everything. As accomplished as Bill Gates is, as much as he and Melinda have achieved with their Foundation, and as much as he has succeeded over the course of his life, winning too many awards and honors to list, there is no chance I would follow everything Gates has done, trying to directly transpose it onto my life. I like my life the way it is, and I have dreams of my own that are nothing like the dreams of any other accomplished person.

On the other hand, analyzing a person's successes, the actions they took, and the responses those actions brought about is a useful way to get a holistic perspective of what one should do and what one should stay away from. There is no need for me to imitate everything to the last detail. You should not either.

Instead, look to the individual characteristics that appeal to you across a multitude of people and discover why those things appeal to you. A number of things appeal to me about Bill Gates. Many things also appeal to me about Steve Jobs, Jack Ma, Bill Clinton, Barack Obama, and, yes, even Donald Trump. (Not everything about someone is bad.) Bill Gates has some qualities that I would emulate, but not all.

One thing that has impressed me and made me consider how I do things myself is the way that Bill Gates prioritizes a task at hand and does whatever it takes to get it done. That is one of the characteristics I have started to see in many people who are highly successful. Whether or not they are comfortable admitting what could be seen as unflattering, people who are successful will do anything they have to in order to get what they want.

There is one thing I would most like to emulate about Bill Gates, more than anything else. What comes naturally to Bill Gates is his empathy for the world in general. Gates' successes are innately linked to it. I am not much into software or building companies, but, for me, the idea of caring for others and looking out for others makes all the difference in the world. When you combine that with the intelligence to do something about it, the result can be explosive.

Putting aside whatever people may think about Bill Gates and Microsoft, something that anyone can appreciate is the way the company revolutionized the world. And in Gates' mind, he was the one to do it. I tend to agree with that.

Certain people can just make specific things happen. There were things Bill Gates was able to do with the launch of the IBM PC that, I believe, no one else could. Only Gates could have done what he did with the operating system that he bought from the original developers. Only he could have made Windows happen. Were it not for Gates' tenacity in getting the products to market, who knows where we would be today in terms of personal computing. Similarly, it is because of the specific talents and legacy of Steve Jobs that Apple sits at the apex of company value. And were it not for Howard Schultz, it's not likely that Starbucks would be around every corner around the world.

When you know that you are the one to make something happen, you owe it to the universe to do everything in your power to get it done. Bill Gates does that, day in and day out, even after leaving the day-to-day operations of the largest software company in the world.

Imagine if you fought tooth and nail to do everything that you set out to do. Imagine the successes all of you, each and everyone one of you, could become.

That is what success is all about. If you have a vision of yourself changing the world, get moving on that vision and don't stop no matter what. Don't be worried about the speed limit. Don't worry about chaffing up against someone. don't worry about dumpster diving to find what you are looking for. It is all about how passionate you are. Just go out and do it. One of the things that I admire about Bill Gates is that he never stops—not even to meet Warren Buffet.

When young Bill Gates first started using computers heavily, he was allowed to access the computers at his school. They had a deal with a local computer company where the kids could use a certain amount of the server time that the company wasn't using. Few kids thought that was much fun, so they didn't take up the opportunity. Bill, on the other hand, jumped at it, and started using the server time to do as much as he could. In fact, he overused the server time and the company started to bill him for it. To access it for free and avoid having to pay for the server time, Bill tried to find a way into the accounting system at the office to get the Admin password. Paul Allen, his high school friend and later co-founder of Microsoft, helped in the effort. Together they managed to get into the accounts and got the password. Before long, the company discovered what they had done and booted them both out of the system. It is just another case of Bill doing whatever it took to do what he needed to do.

Hesitation is a luxury the successful have no time for. When you have something within your grasp, you need to jump on it and worry about the possible consequences later. When you have risk, you should mitigate it to the best of your abilities before you get going, but don't let the risk stop you from moving forward.

Bill Gates worked hard at the things he wanted to do, and didn't allow the time he had to slip by. In fact, the reason he left Harvard the way he did to set up Microsoft wasn't because he imagined there were millions waiting to be made—it was that he knew the best way forward was to get started.

***

Chapter 5 Clarity

"As we look ahead into the next century, leaders will be those who empower others."

Bill Gates

The first comment Bill Gates made after meeting Warren Buffet, and having a long conversation that lasted into the wee hours, was that Buffet had an unusual sense of clarity. Buffet could see how the world works. Bill Gates has the same gift, and that is the real reason the two of them became fast friends, and that is the reason each has dominated in his respective field. It was with that same clarity that he recognized a kindred spirit in Warren Buffet.

Gates' clarity is the reason he is able to do things most only dream of. His intense focus gives him that clarity, without which he wouldn't have the certainty about what he does. If you ask how Gates could quit school so close to graduation, considering how risk-averse he is, and how much he hates failure, the answer is that he was extremely clear about what he intended to accomplish, and he was extremely clear on what he needed to do to accomplish it.

Without that clarity, nothing comes. If you have been working all your life but you find it difficult to move beyond your current life, then I would bet my bottom dollar that you have a problem with clarity.

Clarity is a critical element for Bill Gates and Warren Buffet, and for others like Elon Musk and Bill Clinton— all legendary for what they have accomplished. They are all known even more for the things they have been able to do even in the middle of seemingly debilitating distractions. For them, those distractions become invisible. For Bill Gates, anything that gets in the way of his accomplishing the tasks at hand becomes virtually invisible.

Clarity is both a physiological condition and a psychological one. Many people who spend their time thinking, as Bill did as a kid, are the ones who get to understand and practice clarity. It's not enough to understand what clarity is; it is essential that you practice it.

In my other books on meditation and mindfulness, we talk at length about all the Zen-like qualities and mindfulness, but, in essence, all that mindfulness and meditation is designed to do and to implant is the clarity of who you are, where you are, and what you are doing. That is the essence of all mindfulness training. Deep down, every one of us knows what we need to do, but most of us are so distracted that we need to clear away the distractions to find clarity.

But, for someone like Bill Gates, clarity is even more than just clearing away distractions. It's about not even noticing the distractions in the first place because he is so tuned in and drilled into the point he has focused on. Building the world's largest software company from scratch isn't something that happens by luck or accident. You must relentlessly pursue and painstakingly nurture it. You can only do that when you have both clarity and focus, flip sides of the same coin.

***

Chapter 6 A Strong Mind

"Success is a lousy teacher. It seduces smart people into thinking they can't lose."

Bill Gates

Those who achieve a lot in life typically do so with the aid of a strong mind. It is a prerequisite to being able to handle the challenges presented on the path to success. Without a strong mind, the effort needed becomes relatively insurmountable. A strong mind is more than one attribute; it exists on multiple planes. Whether an Elon Musk or Jack Ma, an Ivy League grad or someone who has barely passed their entrance exams, the measure of their mind is more than academic test scores and institutional certifications.

From childhood, Bill Gates showed signs of superior mental faculties. On one occasion when he was 11, his

Sunday School assignment was to memorize the Book of Matthew—that's about 2000 words. The teacher gave that assignment every year to the confirming class. The incentive was a trip to the Space Needle for dinner. When the time came, with lots of starts-and-stops, misquotes, and jumbled passages, all the students did their best to recite the 2,000 word gospel. Then, it was Bill's turn. To everyone's surprise, he belted out the full 2,000 words without a single error, hesitation or reservation.

Consider for a moment, the power of Bill's mind to be able to memorize those passages. And consider that at age eight he had already breezed through the entire World Encyclopedia. I had one of those when I was eight too, but it took me more than two years to get through it—and that was with the not-so-gentle-prompting of my father.

The ability to memorize is not reserved for a few people. If you try it, and are willing to put in the effort, you will find that, in time, you will be able to memorize as well. Learning to memorize is not going to make you successful, but it will sharpen your mind. The ability to memorize not only expands your mind's abilities, but also develops your will power to focus your mind on one thing at a time without having to ward off distractions.

Gates got through his years at Harvard because he could flawlessly remember everything he read, something that helped him to bridge the gap when it came time for exams. Harvard was just not the challenge he needed. He didn't have to make an effort to get through his classes—memory came naturally to him. On the other hand, programming became a passion for him because it required solving and it provided instant results. He could see the code he needed and manipulate it to do what he wanted.

Bill Gates was always able to apply a singular focus to anything he was doing—whether it was programming or memorizing his Sunday School homework. His mind was powerful but also crystal clear. Combining those two traits produces a person who can see things at a whole different level than those who haven't trained their minds.

It wasn't just about memorizing or doing homework—when Gates set his sights on something, he was persistent and never backed off till it was done—even if it meant diving into dumpsters. When Bill Gates was still in school, he and Paul Allen decided they needed more information on a computer company and wanted to see what the company was working on, so they went to the company's office complex one night. There, Paul boosted Bill (who was much smaller and lighter) into the dumpster. They did this repeatedly, finding all sorts of little treasures, including the source code to the operating system that ran the DEC computer.

Gates relentlessly pursued what he wanted—and that was the way he did things every day. That is characteristic of a man who would go to the ends of the earth to get anything that he wants.

Bill Gates pursued his future wife, Melinda, with the same persistence. The first time he asked her out, she said no. The way he asked reveals a lot about who he was, brimming with confidence. When he bumped into her, he did a mental check of his calendar and knew he had a slot open two weeks from that day, and so he asked her out for two weeks later. She said no, stating that she had no idea what she'd be doing at that time. That was probably an excuse as her real feelings were that she didn't want to be dating the boss. It was uncomfortable, but she did think he was a funny guy and not too bad to be around. After she turned down the invitation, and they had each returned to their respective offices, he called her on the phone and, this time, told her that he was free that night and asked her out again. She agreed.

Bill does not know how to stop, does not know how to quit, and can't take no for an answer. He always gets what he wants. There is no such thing as hesitating for Bill Gates. He doesn't even consider that something's impossible or that it might be a struggle.

That's a quality that I would like to emulate, but I am the kind of person that will think an idea to death before moving on it, by which point it's usually too late. Bill Gates, on the other hand, never hesitated and never slowed down. That, I have come to realize, is a person with a strong mind/ It takes a strong mind to have that kind of confidence in the outcome of their endeavors.

When you combine this mental strength with fearlessness, what you find is someone who will not stop until they have achieved what they have set out to do. When was the last time you went after something—and were relentless until you got it? And I mean something substantial. I don't know about you, but it's been quite a while for me.

***

Chapter 7 Fearless

"Fear is only as deep as the mind allows."

Ralph Waldo Emerson

Right after the clarity that comes from having a strong mind, the characteristic that most defines Bill Gates is the ability to move forward without fear. Don't get me wrong, he has his fears—but it's not about doing or going after the next goal. Gates' fears are about going backwards or not moving forward. His fears are Stoic in nature.

The Stoics have an interesting approach to being successful. Among the values they subscribe to, one is the practice of looking at what's behind you and keeping a healthy sense of fear so that you keep moving forward. The way they do that is by looking at where they are and being thankful for what they have and the opportunities that provides, and then reminding themselves that it can all be gone in a second. Bill Gates has a healthy sense of the notion that it could all be gone in a second. It is also the driving force of every success story I have seen, from Cesar Augustus to Cesar Marcus to Warren Buffet.

The idea is to be fearless going forward and fearful of staying stagnant. The idea is to be fearless in trying and failing, and to be totally afraid of not having the guts to try. You, too, can be fearless—fearless in the same way Bill Gates was when he pitched the operating system owned by another company to IBM and sealed the deal.

Bill Gates was also physically unafraid. Water-skiing is his favorite thing in the world, and he broke his leg doing it. When he got back home in a cast that evening, he didn't make a big deal of it. He was under strict orders to keep the cast on for a specific amount of time, but he didn't listen. His singular focus was to get back on the skis, so he yanked off the cast—with his legs still black and blue—and he got back to it. He wasn't afraid of the pain or the consequences.

Truly successful people aren't afraid because they know that, when the time comes to face a challenge, they have the resources to do it. Jack Ma (Alibaba) was the same way, as was Steve Jobs (Apple), and Elon Musk (Tesla). Elon Musk's trek from South Africa to the United States via Canada is a story of fearlessness you really should read about.

To be clear, I don't suggest you completely abolish all sense of fear. I don't even think it is possible, but if you could, don't. Instead, look at the fearlessness of achievers. They are fearless because they calculate each move in real time. They are not stuck in indecision as they try an idea or an inspiration. They are fearless not because they do not understand the risk but because they know how to handle and mitigate that risk.

It was the same when Bill left Harvard, and the same when Elon left South Africa. It may have seemed like they were blindly pursuing a hair-brained scheme or a Hail Mary, but that wouldn't be how they saw it. They saw an inspired vision of what the future is—not some fantastical pie in the sky, but an idea that had true merit and a desire that was spot on. They were not fantasizing about golden towers in the sky and sail boats in the Mediterranean. They were planning a rigorous path that would allow them to cultivate and sow the seeds of success.

When you have clarity, you can be fearless because you can see where you are going. You are never afraid of what you can see, you are only petrified of what you can't see.

You may see at the tech industry as something alien, but Bill Gates didn't—he was immersed in it. It was his natural element. He knew it best—he was an expert at it and a genius to boot. He could see what was coming. In fact, he was not just able to see what was going to happen, he was part of the reason some of those things happened.

At that level, it becomes a different game. Don't wait to get there to play the game. Start playing the game now—so that you can get there.

***

Chapter 8 Philanthropy

"To me, global poverty is a humanitarian issue. People are dying, and we can save them – and that ought to be enough."

William Henry Gates Sr

There is a difference between a donation, charity, and philanthropy. Most of us make donations on a fairly regular basis. Giving to a charity based on its focus and reach is also something many of us do. But being a philanthropist is not something most of us are able to do or have even thought about doing.

While there is still a lot of little Bill left in this sixty-something-year-old, a lot has changed since the events you have read about in this book, but much has stayed the same. For instance, his perspective of risk remains different than the way most of us perceive it, while his reflections on failure have become more Stoic than they were when he resigned himself to losing at poker in college.

Bill Gates, and many super-contributors like him, find satisfaction in knowing they have touched the lives of many in a positive and constructive way. The more you contribute, the happier you become because that is the most fundamental circuitry of the human purpose.

It's not about making deals and getting the better of the other person. It's not about ravaging the earth and profiting from it. Bill Gates has been about mutual benefit and growth. He moved to enable an entire generation, and that generation serves as the foundation for generations to come. He may not have thought about it in those terms, but that is what his efforts have produced.

When we are inspired to do something, and we combine our talents and interests to do it, we never really know how far it will take us, or where it might take the rest of humanity for that matter. What clouds that is talk of money. Considering the profit you plan to make is fine if you are looking to stay in business, but you shouldn't stop at that.

***

Chapter 9 To Infinity and Beyond

"The Internet is becoming the town square for the global village of tomorrow."

Bill Gates

The books I write about thinkers, leaders, and achievers are based on significant research and analysis. I use a matrix to qualitatively and quantitatively reduce the person I am studying into bite-sized chunks, and use the 80/20 rule—well, it is really more like 90/10—because I have observed that 10% of the man accounts for about 90% of his success.

One of the metrics I use to distill the person to their critical 10% is the finite-infinite matrix in which I consider the way the person views his place in the grand scheme of things. If you haven't read any of my other books, let me quickly describe this matrix and what it does.

The finite-infinite matrix is about matching your internal clock to your actions. There are two kinds of people. One type is the person who is more attuned to the finite measure, and the other is the person who is more tuned to the infinite measure.

It's not whether you are finite or infinite that determines how successful you become, but rather it is how closely you match your own internal rhythm. If you are a finite character, you need to take finite actions and behave in the way that works in the finite world. If you are an infinite person, and you take steps that mirror your infinite nature, you will be successful. The problem arises when you are a finite person but you take steps of an infinite nature. Likewise, if you are an infinite person, you should not do things appropriate for the finite person.

Success is typically determined by how well you do the things that are part of this dimension of your nature. When you see and do things according to your finite-infinite profile, then you will undoubtedly become a success.

This world, however, throws a twist at us. It is designed and made for those who are finite in their personality.

So, just what is a finite personality?

A finite personality is a person who looks at things according to a measurable scale. They look at weekly reviews, quarterly projections, annual revenue, and income, all the benchmarks that can be expressed in finite terms. Even customer service can be expressed in finite terms according to a measurable scale. All these scales and goals are designed to feed the finite personality.

On the other hand, the infinite personality is a person who cannot and will not comprehend the finite numbers, instead looking toward the long term impact of doing something. For instance, if you were to give an infinite person the numbers on why it is okay to burn fossil fuel, they would turn around and look at the issue in a way that cannot be measured and tell you that it does not make sense.

Finite personalities are typically IQ-driven (intelligence quotient), while infinites are typically EQ-driven (emotional quotient). Steve Jobs, for instance, had an infinite personality, and it can be seen in the way he went about designing and looking for the perfect refinements in his product.

A real indicator of a person's personality type is whether they can see the value in the unseen and indefinable elements as easily as they see the value of the parts that can be seen or measured.

When Steve Jobs first got together with Steve Wozniac to create the first Apple computer, Jobs told the guys putting the boards together to arrange them neatly in an organized way. They were confused because the "box" was to be sealed up. No one would see the arrangement of the chips, but Jobs said that he would know. He even made each engineer put their name on the board.

Bill Gates, on the other hand, is a finite person, as revealed in the way he managed his companies and manages his foundation.

Finite and infinite refer to more than just the horizon of one's thinking. It's about the elements a person instinctively prioritizes. When you remain consistent with your priorities, you find that success becomes inevitable.

For instance, the infinite person who is looking to build a long-term engagement with the customer is going to have the habit of fixing things and making them look aesthetically pleasing even under the hood. If that kind of person is asked to slap things together, they will eventually feel drained and unproductive and will lose motivation. On the other hand, the finite person who is looking to make this quarter's numbers is going to overlook whatever does not contribute to that goal and move on to what does.

Have you heard of the 80/20 rule? (The 80/20 rule or the Pareto Principal states that 80% of the results are generated by 20% of the inputs.) However, the rule is only half true because the 80/20 rule applies only to the finite personality. If you are an infinite person, following the 80/20 rule will not work for you; in fact, it will bring you down. The reason a creator of a rule like this believes it works, and will swear by it, is that it works for them. When it works for them, they logically think it will work for everyone. What is overlooked by the creators of such rules is the underlying personality of the person. For some people, rules like the 80/20 just will not work.

You just need to understand who you are. Many people instinctively follow their gut and do what is best for themselves. Parents can make the mistake of forcing their kids to conform to the standards set by schools and the whole academic infrastructure. That ends up forcing the kid to take on a finite personality even though they are wired differently. This is the reason for having so many drop outs and failures—or at least one of the reasons.

Jack Ma (Alibaba) is a classic case of an infinite person in a finite world. This mismatch is the reason he was rejected from schools and couldn't even get a job at KFC. Now he is China's second richest person, with a company that holds the record for the largest IPO day stock value. He found his groove—he started living an infinite life in his own infinite world.

On the other hand, Bill Gates is a finite person who does everything in the now and here. His need for speed, his need for instant results, his need for numbers and trials are all strong indications that he is a person who performs best in the finite world. The Gates manage their foundation by the numbers, and they are very good at it. Remember, one personality type is no better or worse than the other. Finite personalities are great and so are infinites. You just need be loyal to your profile. Bill Gates is.

To understand your own personality, you can read about these successful men, and you will begin to get a practical understanding of the finite-infinite matrix. You can look at men like Steve Jobs, Jack Ma, Richard Branson, and Elon Musk, and start to see their traits and where they fall into the personality groups. As soon as each man found his groove according to his infinite or finite nature, things started to work for him.

Conclusion

"Life is not fair; get used to it."

Bill Gates

If you were expecting a chronological order of events in the life of William Henry Gates, this was not the book for you. This book has been about a man and the events that shaped him and the people who were responsible for how he reacted to those events.

Of course, the number one influence on Bill Gates was Bill Gates, Sr., his dad. Bill Gates was influenced by all the things his father did and the way his father did them—from the technology that his father was so interested in to the philanthropy that Senior knew to be the best source of lasting satisfaction.

Bill Gates' ambition, intelligence, empathy, immense focus, ability to ferret out essentials, and his ability to negotiate and design documents that reflected that agreement were all already part of him as a child and remained part of him as he grew up to become the successful man we see today.

My first exposure to Bill Gates left me a little uncomfortable. The combination of my youth, and the righteousness that inevitably comes with it, combined with a lack of information, left me unimpressed with the man that stood behind the operating system that, for the past quarter century, has been on a majority of the world's computers. Truth be told, I am not a fan of Windows, but I respect what it has done and how far it has gone.

Since then, I've realized that Bill Gates was not in it for the money. Bill Gates may have had his moment of going overboard for a while, splashing his money around, but that passed quickly. Most of his money now goes to the foundation where he has also pledged even more in his succession documents. Warren Buffet, who is arguably Bill Gates' closest friend, also donated his fortunes to the Bill and Melinda Foundation. Together, the two men have gone around trying to convince the world's wealthy to follow their example and give up their wealth for charity.

Bill and Warren have both left instructions that around 90% of their wealth will go to charities doing research to help develop the nations that are in such dire straits we cannot even begin to imagine it. From agricultural genetics to reproductive health in some of the poorest third world countries, Bill and Melinda have personally been involved in determining how the research is funded and how the solutions are structured.

Ultimately, Bill Gates is proof that we live in a world where we are all connected, and we are responsible for the way we develop and the path we choose. Bill chose to follow a focused path that resulted in a tremendous contribution to the world we all live in. Whether you agree with his methods or not, or monopolistic tendencies, the net result, in the end, was one that was good for all.

He has given as much as he earned, and it was evident from day one that it was never about the money. It was about the accomplishment. A person who is in it for the money will not only cheat and swindle if things do not go his way, he will also subconsciously find ways to lavishly tell the world how rich he is (which is usually an exaggeration). In Bill's case, his philanthropic efforts and the life he lives reveals that it has never been about the fame and fortune so much as it has been about seeing the objective in his head come to fruition.

Bill Gates has a unique intelligence, with knowledge that goes beyond a nerd's understanding of technology and programming. Not only could he memorize and program, but he could also weigh everything and understand things at their most fundamental level. He could also understand the movements of business and society. While Gates is a highly cerebral and immensely logical person, not interested in niceties, he is concerned with practical needs of community and humanity.

Bill Gates is indeed a unique person, as you and I are. We are all unique.

***

I hope you have taken away some interesting insights from this book. I hope that somewhere in its lines you find the note that resonates with you and awakens your spirit to gain the clarity you need to accomplish all the things you have thought about. I hope that it brings you happiness and that you find the path that lights up your soul and animates your existence.

May you find all that you want in life. Compare yourself to no one, but just move forward improving on your yesterday's self.

***

If you enjoyed this book, I would be forever grateful if you could leave a review on Amazon. Reviews are the best way to help your fellow readers find the books worth reading. Thanks in advance!

Make sure to check out the next book in this 'Billionaire Visionaries' series:

Jack Ma: A Lesson in Trust, Honor, and Shared Prosperity

Made in the USA
Monee, IL
17 December 2019